*"911…What's your Diversity?"*

*A Pocket Guide for Law Enforcement Diversity Issues*

By:

Michael A. Crawford

# Table of Contents

## Preface

Growing up in Southern Louisiana, I have seen the issue of race relations regarding Law Enforcement move in such a manner that simply guided me to become an Instructor for First Responders specifically towards teaching Cultural Diversity for Law Enforcement. This book is a culmination of my own perspectives, analytics from both citizens and those that identify themselves as Law Enforcement, and from teaching on the subject matter around the state of Louisiana for over the past 10 years.

\*\*\*

## Acknowledgements

### -*To my parents*

To my parents, Andrew and Carol, thank you both for showing me that God loves all of us for who we are and we should always treat others the same. You all raised my brother, Jason, and I to treat people with respect and to always show love and compassion in helping others. You both worked hard to provide us with the best educational opportunities, a nice home to grow up in and the opportunity to be ourselves and to make friends and relationships with people from all walks of life.

*-To my daughters*

MacKenzie and Hannah, you both are equally the apple of my eye! I am blessed beyond measure to have beautiful daughters like the two of you. Unlike some homes and working families, you both share your daily lives with me and your mother and in turn have helped me to see life in these days and times as hopeful and promising. I hope and pray that as you both grow into remarkable women, that the troubles of this world will not be your troubles and that PEACE, LOVE, JOY, RESPECT, and CHRISTANITY still reigns!

## -To my wife

The reason this book exist is because of you sweetheart! Erica, you have been the force behind my strength in this profession and behind every "brainy" idea (good or bad) that I have come up with. From daily conversations to late night pillow talks about life, my job, my career, and why this book was so important to write and publish. You have been there from day one, cheering me along. Watching me leave the home, in uniform and praying for my safe return for over 20 years. And for this I say, "Thanks and I love you".

*-To my brothers and sisters in "Blue"*

It is my sincere hope and prayer that this book is simply a resource to help within your daily duties with the many people we "Serve and Protect".  Our job is often hard at times and I ask that you look at the issues of Diversity with an open mind and at the end of the day, remember why we took our oaths. **Godspeed!!!**

## Intention

Listen! This book is not one that should not redirect anyone from their agency's Policy and Procedures when it comes to how to treat people. It is my intention that this book be another "tool" that accompanies the officer/ first responder in their daily duties. It can be carried in the unit, left at a duty station, and be used as appropriate reading material while on duty. Again, this book is my opinion on matters that we all come in to contact with, my life experiences, and my conversations with fellow LEO's. Whether it be in an educational setting or just through conversations with the general public about issues that affect both sides of the coin.

# CHAPTER 1 –

## "WHAT IS DIVERSITY"?

So what is Diversity?  Have you ever just stopped for a minute to really understand what Diversity is or means?  Or are you where I was many years ago thinking that it simply meant, "Knowing that other people are different" or "making sure I don't violate their rights"?  Well if you thought both, I still believe that we are on the right track especially being in Law Enforcement.  But I can tell you that it's more than just these two assumptions and that understanding Diversity is one of the key elements in being successful in this profession.

Without a knowledge of understanding of how and why other people do things, reacting a certain way or have certain beliefs, our job as LEO's can and will become increasingly harder.

In order to fully appreciate where people are coming from and why it's important to have a greater understanding to provide the best public service possible, one would need to not only experience another culture, but possibly be from that particular group. Although many agencies around the United States have broadened their search, training and retention on having officers that mirror and reflect such diverse groups, it comes as no secret that many issues with Diversity come from people who are in fact, not the same.

So here we are back to the same question posed earlier and that is, "What is Diversity"?  In short on an academic level the answer is, "an instance of being composed of different elements or qualities", but I believe that there is more to it.  I believe that the mere essence of the word beginning with the first two letters, "di" which means to "separate, have contrast with, differences" all state that something is in fact different.  Different? Yes, different!  The appreciation that we as people come from all walks of life or in fact not the same, makes us all diverse beings.  I have often said in my classes that,

*"I am not asking anyone in this room to think of diversity as a small puppy or kitten that you've found abandoned. Where you feel compelled to pick it up, show it love and attention and to stroke its' back from a level of trust and safety. All I ask is that you acknowledge that it is there and to handle the situation as a LEO who's Sheriff, Chief or Superintendent was standing close by and observing.  And quite frankly as if the person you truly respect the most, while either growing up or currently, was watching you today.  How would you handle it?  What would you do?"*

Don't ignore the fact that people are different and we are different for various reasons.  Whether it be our family make-up, our own adversities and experiences or simply how we see the world through television, newspapers, the media, and the abundance of Social Media Networks".  Bottom line, if someone needs our help regardless of their diverse issues, it our duty to provide them with the best professional service possible.

## CHAPTER 2 –

## "STEREOTYPING VS. PROFILING"

One of the biggest things in modern day that has become a major topic is that we as a country have evolved to being a "Post-Racial Era". But is this a true statement or factual? And if so, by whose terms or eyes are we seeing this change in policy through? Although we in Law Enforcement get hammered and sued daily across the globe for acts of Stereotyping and Profiling, I am going to go out on a limb and say that they are one in the same. Being that we are servants of the public and representatives of government whether in small capacities like rural departments or in large federal agencies, we are really no different than other professions that deal or interact with people on a daily basis.

When a Cadet is in the Academy, we teach him or her that Racial Profiling is wrong, unethical, not moral, and is subject to law suits, penalties, and possible termination if found guilty of performing. But aren't we all GUILTY?  We as American Law Enforcement often cover up the obvious with words like, "stereotyping" or "labeling", but for all intense purposes, most successful LEO's will give credit to "Profiling".

So let's take a quick observation; What if I gave members of Law Enforcement and the public these phrases?  Who would you say meets the descriptions and why?


*A mass shooting*

*A troubled past*

*A person who kept to themselves*

*A person who seemed awkward at times*

*A person who lived with older parents or relatives*


Here's another one:


*-A drive-by shooting*

*-A rough life in a bad neighborhood*

*-A product of a single mother*

*-A person who didn't do well in school*

*-A person who had many siblings, some*

*by different fathers*

What were your first thoughts about both of these examples?  Did you assume? Did you base any of your thoughts on your own interactions, your own life?  Or did you use recent media outlets or social media to help determine the kind of person by race, demographics, and by gender?

Let me help you on this one...............ADMIT IT! That's right, OWN UP TO IT!  We may not be able to say it on the scene, in a written report, in an interview/interrogation, and especially in court, **but**

**we do Profile**, **we do Stereotype** and quite frankly, **we are not going to stop**.  The mere notion of trying to not look at what we deem as the "obvious" cannot be removed from our psyche.  Often times when we are looking for a person of interest or suspect, we look for the characteristics of the crime. We look at the location, the method, weapons used, and motive.  And depending on these factors and more, we try to determine if the person was male or female, or White, Black, Asian, Hispanic or any other race.  *Oh and by the way, this book is for the working Enforcer, I'm simply not doing the "Caucasian", "African-American", and etc.…...*

So is there a difference between "Stereotyping vs. Profiling"?  I'll let you be the judge on this one.

## CHAPTER 3 –

## "THE USE OF WORDS"

*"Sticks and Stones may break my bones, but*

*words will never hurt"- Unknown*

*(The Christian Recorder, March 1862)*

Not sure who came up with this phrase, but it's one of the biggest lies I was ever taught. Words do hurt and the *sting* of how it's delivered may last a lifetime. Even the most strong willed, determined, and built tough person will ponder on the words that someone may have called them or used to describe their actions, their looks, and even their character.

I am reminded of a phrase that former First Lady Michelle Obama once said, *"When they go low, you go high"*. This phrase at the time was given as a mantra for all of us. Not just for blacks, for females, for a specific socio-class of people, but it simply meant, when people try to bring you down, don't lay there in wait, but to hold up your head and move forward to higher ground. It's called, treating people right!

Another incident that comes to mind is that of the late American Icon, Prisoner of War, and U.S. Senator, John McCain. In his bid to run for President of the United States back in 2015, then candidate, Donald Trump was recorded during an interview stating that he did not consider Senator

McCain to be a war hero. And that *"He's not a war hero. He's a war hero because he was captured. I like people that weren't captured."* This was eluding to McCain's five years of being held captive as a prisoner of the Vietnam War. It was soon after Trump's comment about McCain that he was asked on a news outlet what he thought about the statement and if he felt that Trump owed him an apology. McCain's answer was as diplomatic as they come, "no". He went on to say that Trump should apologize to heroes, people of valor, families and so on.

What you say, the conversations you have in the privacy of your home, the talks you have with your close friends, are in fact **your** business however, as a public servant and more importantly as a Law Officer, we must always be mindful of the words we use.  Words such as:

| | | |
|---|---|---|
| *Boy* | *Girl* | *Wetback* |
| *Chinc (Chink)* | *Wigger* | *Honkey* |
| *Dike (Dyke)* | *Nigga* | *Nigger* |
| *Gal* | *Cracker* | *Coon* |
| *Faggot* | *Punk* | *Fat* |
| *You People* | *Crackhead* | *Bitch* |
| *Trailer Trash* | *Those People* | *Shuga* |
| *White Trash* | *Them People* | |

These words have become a part of people's dialect for years, some decades.  There is probably not and American, of age, who does not know the meaning and usage of each word that was listed. How did we get to these words and how did they become defamatory?  Why are some of the words okay for one race to use and not the other?  Why do people get offended by these words if they don't apply to them?

We must, as professionals, stick to the basics when it comes to our vocabulary.  If we are talking to a male, we should use, *"Sir", "Young Man", "Gentleman"* or a female, *"Ma'am", "Young Lady", or "Ladies".*  Even when the situation becomes rough, confrontational or physical, we must always remain professional as we just do not only represent ourselves.  Our families, our communities, and our agencies are all depending on us to be the person of reason, the professional, and the keeper of peace.

We know that words can incite an already volatile event and even a calm situation, we must in fact, use this powerful tool carefully, just the same as we would using a defensive tool on our duty rigs. In the days of cellphones, cameras, social media, and now, body cameras, just about everything we do and say is being recorded and used later when necessary.  Be vigilant, be careful, and like many of us were taught in elementary school, *"Be Courteous"*.

**Remember, you are being watched!**

## CHAPTER 4 –

## "RACE AND CULTURE"

I can remember when I was in middle and high school going to regular Doctor's appointments and having to sit in the waiting rooms.  Partly because I suffered as a kid with a chronic case of dermatitis and to the thanks of my parents, they tried every remedy and every doctor.  But while sitting in the waiting rooms, I often became bored as cellphones were still a luxury and they came in the form of a "bag phone" that you could tote around. I turned to the old standard, that's right, a magazine that you actually had to read or at least look at the pictures.  It was then that I became intrigued in what I saw in the magazines, especially "National Geographic". I noticed that the magazine would capture events all around the world, it would have pictures of rare artifacts, exotic animals, and the list goes on. However, the magazine would often show indigenous people from around the world and unless it was just me, when it came to the continent of Africa, the pictures often showed the bodies of Africans, mostly the women, topless and very often the kids were generally not clothed themselves. Let me be clear, I am not saying that this was or is a form of "racial or biasness", but one that speaks to the thought process of some as to what people still consider "race" and "culture" in this day and age. When I hear modern day people say things like, "they act like monkeys", "they should go back to Africa", or "black women's bodies have big butts", it tells me that they don't respect culture.


Race and culture define who we all are as people, as human beings, and as races of people who all bleed the same color blood. Race is primarily an "outward" look and it gets so confused and labeled with the actions of people. Culture is simply a way of how we think and behave based upon how we were raised both in the home and in the communities in which we live. So when I hear people talk about culture, a great percentage of the time, the person speaking is in the right area of assumption, but often will go wrong when they include things or ideas that are incorrect in generalization.

I once was on vacation with my family in Texas and when stopping for fuel, I went inside to purchase some snacks for the kids.  When I finally got to the counter, I noticed a young black male working behind the counter, probably in his early to mid-twenties.  Here's where I went wrong, I assumed on looks alone that the cashier was "black" and when I started to ask questions about directions to a water park, I soon noticed that he had a thick accent and it sounded like "Spanish". Well I tell you that day I was thrown off base and in reality, began to check my own understanding of assumptions and perceptions in regard to race and culture.  Not that anything was wrong with his speaking abilities, but I was prepared to hear the voice of a black man (not sure what that sounds like, but I believe you get the picture) and to my amazement, it wasn't such.

Another scenario I use in my classes when it relates to culture is food!  We all love food and we especially love food that is prepared to our liking and that pleases the palate.  In each class no matter the size of the class or the make-up of the audience, I offer this sort of game as an ice breaker if you will.  And I ask these series of questions:

**What do Black people eat?**

**Answers:  Chicken, watermelon, Soul Food, etc.**

*What do Asian people eat?*

*Answers:  Rice, noodles, "cat",*

*"dogs", "rats", etc.*

*What do Hispanic people eat?*

*Answers:  Beans, corn and flour*

*tortillas, peppers, etc.*

*What do White people eat?*

*Answers:  All of the above!*

I do this obviously for a reason. I play on the stereotypes that we all have heard and shamefully some have participated in saying.  I often allow the class to laugh and comment, with respect to each other, in a playful way to see that we as people are often "racists" towards food and who consumes it. Afterwards we all as a group come up with ways to make our remarks and generalizations better towards others and their respective cultures.  And the main focus I ask them to walk away with is, *if we as Law Enforcement and First Responders don't improve our abilities on even the smallest levels, how can we expect or request this from the people we serve?*

## CHAPTER 5 –

## "GENDER AND SEXUAL PREFERENCE"

One of the biggest misconceptions that we as LEO's face is that, at times, we treat people differently based on their gender.  And guess what? It's true!  Although we should all follow the "Color of Law" and treat all people equal, human nature and how we are raised seemingly takes center stage on some occasions. This mere subject has been argued in many courtrooms, how the actions of an Officer were altered due to the gender of the subject or offender.  And in another courtroom, a prosecutor may ask the court or jury as to why an Officer didn't use or display "human compassion" in a certain case or incident.  One can't help but to

think of the quote, *"we're dammed if we do and*

*dammed if we don't"*, when it comes to what

actions we take, especially in regard to gender and

sexual preferences.

Males in Law Enforcement generally perform or act

on gender issues more than female enforcers.  One

could argue a plethora of issues as to why, but I will

stick with one that seems to be more prevalent, and

that is, looks!  If a beautiful woman is caught

speeding by a male LEO, this stop could in most

cases could go 50/50.  The offender may be cited

for breaking the law or she could be "left off" with a

courtesy or no infraction simply because she is

pleasing to the eye of the male.  What messes this

scenario up is when a female that may not be attractive to the male officer completes the same violation, the result may lean in percentage to 60/40 or 70/30 as to whether a citation will be issued or not. Is this fair? Isn't the officer allowed to use his discretion per the law? Who's to say? However, those that stick to the law and will cite the offender for their actions never have to worry about this being a factor later down the road.

But let's switch gears for a moment, in some cases the sexual preference of the citizen plays a factor in how we perform our tasks as well. Those citizens that prefer an "alternate lifestyle", that are homosexual, that label themselves as "gay or lesbian", shouldn't they receive the same protections and service as heterosexuals?  Of course the answer without question is, "yes"!  It is imperative that we as LEO's take our oaths seriously and that we do not waiver from it.  Just because a person doesn't practice your preference when it comes to relations and sex, does not mean that we should treat them any different.  I understand that we all have different upbringings, different religious beliefs, and different thought processes about people who are a part of the LGBTQ society, but remember we "Serve and Protect" *ALL* of our citizens.

It is both unprofessional and downright unfair to show signs of discrimination due to someone's preference.  I have often said that I have a problem with flamboyant people. I say this because I think we look at the lifestyle more than the individual and whether you are heterosexual, bi-sexual, homosexual, or however you deem yourself, a person that seeks the attention of others in a loud and flashy way is the root of my apprehensions with them, not who they sleep with or what kind of relationship they are in. We should also watch our physical actions, facial expressions, and most importantly what we say while being professionals. Just because you don't agree with their choice, doesn't mean the department or agency you work for does either. They, for the most part, will not pay you to disrespect or deny the individual certain rights and privileges that they deserve.

*We should always treat people like we want to be treated! (Maybe even better)*

# CHAPTER 6 –

## "ENCOUNTERING OTHER CULTURES"

Some of us may feel like we are not in charge of the call or situation when coming in to contact with people that represent other cultures. This is mainly because when we show up on a call or scene, we are the people that instruct or direct others on where to go, where to stand, what areas to stay out of, and where to run to safety.  But when we cannot communicate this due to a true language barrier, how then do we stay effective in our roles? As much confidence as you may have, don't be taken back that you do not feel sure of your actions in the moment.  Most of us in Law Enforcement generally display a lot of self-esteem, often times too much, and even those of you who do, may not feel in control like you normally are.  So what's the solution?  How do we overcome a clear language barrier?  I hate to break the news to you, but if don't speak the language, the chances are not in your favor for effective communication.

However, all it not lost and depending on the size of your agency, the diverseness of your department, or if your office has a partnership with community leaders that have resources to assist, this may not be a problem after all.  There is a language that I have found to be most effective and it turns out, we all know it.  And that is Body Language.  We use it to determine if someone may

potentially "bolt and run", we use it to see the
movements of a victim in distress who may not
verbally say it, and we use it to determine if a
person may be armed or not when conducting an
interview or field statement.  So why not use the
same principle when trying to communicate with
other cultures?


One idea that may help you and the people
in your community is to learn and observe what
groups, races, cultures, etc...may be moving into in
the area.  For example, there may be an influx of
citizens who are Russian and speak very little
English.  Why not introduce yourself to them while
on duty or on patrol?  Work on some ways to get
past the initial, "Hello" or "Hi".  We use search

engines all the time when browsing the internet whether we are on our laptops, MDT's, or cell phones. Use the tools at hand to learn ways to say or translate common words and by doing so you will have accomplished two things for sure, a trust or bond with that person or that family and gained a better knowledge base. If you haven't been in Law Enforcement long, you must know that a smart Cop, is an educated Cop. There is nothing wrong with staying on top of issues that affect the people you serve and if especially if that same issue happened in your community. By doing this method of meeting and greeting, a nice way of saying "Community Policing", way before the need for you to respond to a dispatch or call, you will have set the tone, the standard, and have gained some insight that just may benefit you towards possible investigations.

### *Here are some pointers to remember:*

-   Always remember to use body language and safe hand gestures when needed until an interpreter, whether another person in the neighborhood, a family member, or a co-worker arrives. Just remember to keep your hands high and visible, away from your gun belt or duty rig, and to move or gesture in a manner that does not seem aggressive or that scares the person.  If not, you alone may have now contributed to the situation getting worse for both the citizen, yourself, and your co-workers.

- Keep in mind that depending on the culture or ethnicity of the person, you may not be able to have a dialogue or receive a statement.  Not because they do not speak English, but it may just be a cultural custom or tradition.  You may have to speak with the elder of the family, you may have to speak with the man or husband in the relationship first, and don't get bent out of shape if the person talking to you is not making eye contact. For certain cultures and groups, this is a sign of respect and you being the authority on the scene is the sole reason why.

\-   And lastly, dress and appearance often identify who people are in regard to their family make-up, their religious belief, and staying true to their ancestral upbringing. If clothing becomes an issue in a serious situation or incident or pat and frisk is warranted, remember to follow your departmental policy and oh yeah, follow the Law!

## CHAPTER 7 –

## "WHY DID YOU CHOOSE THIS PROFESSION"

There has not been a time in the last 15 or so years that I have been teaching on the subject matter of Diversity, that I have not asked my audience this main question, "Why did you choose to become a Cop"? Depending on the size of the participants and if time permits, I allow this question to be answered by those who do not mind playing along. Some of the answers I get are common answers for the profession,

*"It was a calling", "I wanted to help others", "It (Law Enforcement) runs in my family", "My dad was a Cop", "My brother*

**was or is a Cop", and "I want to Serve**

**and Protect".**

And most recently in the past few years, some of

the responses have been,

**"They were hiring", "I just needed a job",**

**"I've watched cop shows and thought it**

**would be neat to do"," I'm just buying or**

**building my time up to go State or**

**Federal".**

I must admit that I have never in my 20+ years in

Law Enforcement, heard a person say, "I wanted to

be in a position to hurt someone", "I wanted to use

my power to take advantage of people", or "I

wanted to become a Cop because I'm racist and I

wanted a new way of taking rights from people".

Every major television network or premium provider has a hit series drama about Law Enforcement.  These shows often have "A list" actors/actresses and the crime and drama gets more intense with each episode.  However, you find these shows and movies as entertainment, far-fetched, or spot on, the general public often use what they watch as what we should be doing. For dispatchers and those who get dispatched, the complainants or callers seem to think they know how we should be handling their situation, what should be finger printed, or what crime was committed. Which goes to say that we are always being watched, often criticized, and under scrutiny unlike any other profession.  It remains imperative that you remember to give it your best and do simply do what your department or agency ask of you …"Your Job".

Generally most police applicants, rookies, and new hires, are people who what to truly make a difference and truly help their communities, towns, and municipalities. Although there are certain agencies/ departments that offer generous salaries, excellent benefits, and great retirements, not every entity can compete or provide this. Which goes to say, that we all simply do it, not for the money, but because we really want to "Serve and Protect". Whatever your reason, stay true to it as long as it is positive and it continues to represent your agency or department in a good way.

# CHAPTER 8 –

## "YOUR PERSONAL VALUES"

So by now you have read all the chapters and have made it to Chapter 8. Congrats and thank you for taking the time to read this book, whether your purchased it yourself, it was given to you, or your workplace provided it. I must now ask of you to really think hard, really remain open minded, and to really be honest with yourself when answering this question, "What are your personal values"? Have you ever just sat and thought about this question, ever laid in bed or on the sofa and asked yourself this question? What is a deal breaker for you as far as something your value, something that cannot be changed in your life, or something that you have made up in your mind that you would die for, to save, or to keep safe?  What's that one thing that is unwavering or who is so important that if it came down to it, you would have no problem giving all you had or own to keep healthy?


For me, the answer is simple, I declare that I am a Christian!  I serve and worship the Son of God, Jesus Christ, and I am not ashamed to say that HE is my personal Savior!  But the truth is, this is MY choice and the fact that I have taken a solemn oath to "Serve and Protect", doesn't always give me the right to push or influence my opinion or faith on others.  We have to understand that what is of value to you, may not be of value to others.

What seems normal or deserves a normal reaction or response, may not be what the other person needs or understands. You see my friend, we have a job unlike any other, we can see a situation and ask, "You need help", "what's going on", or even, "who are you and what are you doing"? The job of a Law Enforcement Officer allows us to be noisy, questionable, curious, and sometimes judgmental enough to make the right call for the situation.

I ask that you remember how you grew up, where you grew up, and the words or language that was used in your home. What make us all unique is that we are all truly different and that my friend, is okay and doesn't have to be looked at as a bad or negative thing. Remember the oath you took and that we really do more than serve one race, one gender, or creed. We do more than protect those who look like us, share our same skin tone, or share our same religious or social beliefs. We are servants and protectors of all people, whether they like or us or not, it comes with the job and with the job comes the responsibility.

Godspeed to you, great men and women of blue, stay vigilant, stay alert and at all cost, and stay alive! We need you, your departments need you, and most importantly, your family or friends need you.

###